¡Todos a Comer!
A Mexican Food Alphabet Book

Dr. Ma. Alma González Pérez

¡Todos a Comer!

A Mexican Food Alphabet Book

2017 International Latino Book Awards
Best Latino Focused Children's Picture Book

Text and translation copyright © 2017 by Ma. Alma González Pérez

Published in the United States by Del Alma Publications, LLC, Texas
Book design by Maricia Rodríguez & Teresa Estrada
Photography by Del Alma Publications, LLC except for kiosk image © Leigh Thelmadatter.

Front cover: Plate contains fajitas, taco, enchiladas rojas, rice, beans, and guacamole.
Subject: Non-fiction-Mexican food, culture, bilingual, Spanish

Our books may be purchased in bulk for educational use.
Please contact us at delalmapublications@gmail.com.

ISBN-13 978-0-9822422-6-1

Library of Congress Control Number: 2018908873

Printed in China
First Edition

Meeting the Biliteracy Challenges of the Hispanic Learner

For a variety of teaching tools, visit us at www.delalmapublications.com

DEDICATORIA

Dedico este libro a los niños hispanos
de los Estados Unidos
con el gran deseo de que sigan
amando y valorando la cultura de su gente
y, así, legarla a los niños de sus niños.
M.A.G.P.

DEDICATION

I dedicate this book to the Hispanic children
of the United States
with the great desire that they will continue
to love and to cherish the culture of their people
and, thus, pass it on to the children of their children.
M.A.G.P.

The Bilingual Shelf – Todos a Comer! A Mexican Food Alphabet Book is a bilingual, soft-cover English/Spanish alphabet book featuring traditional Mexican cuisine (in mouth-watering, full-color photography!) for each letter of the alphabet. "Uu is for uvas. Grapes are used to prepare salads and desserts. In the Hispanic culture, it is a custom to eat twelve grapes to welcome the new year. Does your family have this custom?" A picture glossary of Mexican cooking utensils rounds out this delightful ABC book, ideal for reading aloud and sharing with young children. - Midwest Book Review

¡Todos a comer! A Mexican Food Alphabet Book is so much fun. It includes one food or dish for each letter of the Spanish alphabet (with the exception of W). The layout of each page consists of a delicious picture with Spanish text on the top and English on the bottom. The photos are colorful and feature some of the most popular dishes in Mexican cuisine. There are history lessons embedded in the short descriptions that will give parents additional topics to discuss. Families with young children should have a growing collection of books at home to be read over and over to their little ones. And for those with children learning to read, a set of alphabet books – or abecedarios – are a must! They allow children to see how letters are used in different ways and how they make up the basis of our language. Alphabet books develop literacy skills and help prepare children to begin the process of learning to read. So it is imporant to have abecedarios that are fun, colorful, and engaging. ¡Todos a comer! does just that. - Mommy Maestra

I read this book with my 7-year-old nephew and he gave it 5 Platypires. He said he enjoyed this book and liked that it was in English and in Spanish. He liked learning about all the different foods from Mexico some of which he has eaten. He said he plans on reading this book to his younger brothers so they can learn as well. Personally, I thought it was fun to read the book in both languages. I also enjoyed learning about all the different foods. I liked how the pictures were all colorful and when we stumbled over a word we could find the translation pretty easily. Overall, I would recommend this book to those who are in a bilingual home. - Platypire Reviews

PREFACIO

La comida mexicana ha trascendido fronteras y ha logrado gran éxito en el mercado de los Estados Unidos. Es por eso que es sumamente importante que los niños de todas las nacionalidades aprendan más sobre los ingredientes y los procedimientos para preparar las muy deliciosas comidas mexicanas.

Es también importante que los niños hispanos, en particular, lean más sobre su cultura para un mayor entendimiento de las muchas contribuciones de sus antepasados a la cultura americana. Por lo tanto, lograrán así más apreciación de su cultura y sentirán más orgullo de sí mismos, de su gente y de su historia.

Este abecedario sobre la comida mexicana puede ser utilizado para la lectura oral o compartida tanto como para la lectura en pareja o independiente. Tiene un doble propósito: desarrollar el conocimiento sobre la comida mexicana y desarrollar el tema y/o la extensión del aprendizaje. Sin embargo, se debe aclarar que este libro es un abecedario y no un diccionario y es por eso que sólo incluye una comida o platillo para cada letra del alfabeto en español excepto la 'ñ' y la 'w' que se usa mayormente en palabras extranjeras. Se han excluído la 'ch' y la 'll' que han sido designadas por la Real Academia Española como diágrofos y no letras. Se le sugiere al maestro(a) o al padre de familia que al leer el libro le pida al niño que provea más ejemplos de otras comidas para cada letra.

Cada descripción de comida es acompañada por una pregunta por la cual se le pueda pedir al alumno una respuesta oral como parte de un desarrollo del idioma oral o como una tarea escrita como respuesta a la lectura. Además, este libro también puede ser utilizado como fuente de referencia sobre la comida mexicana. Más importante aún, es nuestro gran deseo que este libro sea útil para el aula bilingüe y que a la vez también sea de su más completo agrado.

PREFACE

Mexican food has transcended borders and has achieved great success in the United States marketplace. It is, therefore, critically important that children of all nationalities learn more about the ingredients and procedures for preparing the very delicious Mexican dishes.

It is also important that Hispanic children, in particular, read more about their culture for a better understanding of the many contributions of their ancestors to the American way of life. In so doing, they will, thus, gain greater appreciation of their culture and take greater pride in themselves, in their people, and in their history.

This alphabet book on Mexican food may be used as a read-aloud or for shared reading as well as for paired or independent reading. Its purpose is twofold: to build background about Mexican food and to provide further discussion and/or extension of learning. It must be noted, however, that this is an alphabet book, not a dictionary, and as such, it only includes one food or dish for each letter of the Spanish alphabet except the 'ñ' and the 'w' which is mostly used in foreign words. 'Ch' and 'll' are excluded because they have been designated by the *Real Academia Española* as diagraphs and not letters. It is suggested that the teacher or parent ask the child to provide more examples of other foods for each letter.

Each food description is followed by a question which may be used to solicit an oral response as part of an oral language discussion or as a written response to the reading. In addition, this book may be also used as a reference source on Mexican food. Most importantly, we hope that this book will be useful for the bilingual classroom and, at the same time, we greatly hope that you will also enjoy it as well.

Aa es para arroz con pollo.

El arroz con pollo se cuece a vapor. Se sazona con especias, cebolla, chile verde y tomate. Se complementa con frijoles y tortillas.

¿Cocina tu familia el arroz con pollo?

Aa is for arroz con pollo.

Arroz con pollo (chicken with rice) is cooked as a casserole. It is seasoned with spices, onion, green peppers, and tomato. It is complimented with beans and *tortillas*.

Does your family cook *arroz con pollo*?

Bb es para barbacoa.

La barbacoa se cuece en un hoyo por muchas horas. Los tacos de barbacoa son un almuerzo tradicional los domingos.

¿Tiene tu familia esta costumbre los domingos?

Bb is for *barbacoa*.

Barbacoa (pit barbeque) is cooked in a pit for many hours.
Barbacoa tacos are a traditional breakfast on Sundays.
Does your family have this Sunday custom?

Cc es para chocolate.

El chocolate es una bebida muy nutritiva hecha del cacao. Los mayas y los aztecas lo cultivaban antes de la llegada de los españoles a América.

¿Qué otros productos se hacen del cacao?

Cc is for chocolate.

Chocolate is a very nutritious drink made from *cacao* beans. The Mayas and Aztecs cultivated *cacao* before the Spaniards came to America.

What other products are made from *cacao* beans?

Dd es para dulces.

Los dulces mexicanos son muy ricos. La leche quemada es un dulce muy popular. Otros son las obleas, palanquetas y el mazapán.

¿Qué dulces te gustan a ti?

Dd is for *dulces.*

Mexican candy is very rich. *Leche quemada* (boiled milk) is a very popular candy. Others include *obleas, palanquetas,* and *mazapán.*

What candies do you like?

Ee es para enchiladas.

Las enchiladas mexicanas son de queso fresco. Además, hay de queso americano, pollo y de carne. Se les agrega cebolla y salsa para las enchiladas. ¿Cuál es tu enchilada favorita?

Ee is for *enchiladas.*

Mexican *enchiladas* are made with fresh white cheese. There are also *enchiladas* made with American cheese, chicken, and beef. They are topped with onion and *enchilada* sauce. What is your favorite *enchilada*?

Ff es para fajitas.

Las fajitas se cuecen a la parrilla. Se les sazona con especias, cebolla y chile verde. Los tacos de fajita son de tortillas de harina o de maíz.

¿Te gustan los tacos de fajita?

Ff is for *fajitas.*

Fajitas (beef skirts) are cooked on the grill. Spices, onion, and green peppers are added to enhance their flavor. *Fajita tacos* are made with flour or corn *tortillas.*

Do you like *fajita tacos?*

Gg es para guacamole.

El aguacate se muele y luego se le agrega el tomate, cebolla y chile picado. También se le agrega lima para mantener fresco el sabor.

¿Con qué comidas se sirve el guacamole?

Gg is for *guacamole.*

The *aguacate* or avocado is mashed and then diced tomatoes, onion, and *chile* peppers are added. Lime is also added to maintain its freshness.

With what meals is *guacamole* served?

Hh es para horchata.

La horchata es una bebida de verano. Se incluye entre las conocidas aguas frescas de México. Se hace de arroz hervido en leche, azúcar y canela. ¿Has probado la horchata?

Hh is for *horchata.*

Horchata is a summer drink. It is included among the well known *aguas frescas* or natural drinks of Mexico. It is made from rice boiled in milk, sugar, and cinnamon. Have you tasted *horchata*?

Ii es para indígena.

La comida mexicana tiene gran influencia indígena. Las razas indígenas de América cultivaban chile, maíz y frijol mucho antes de la Conquista de México.

¿Qué otras comidas son de origen indígena?

Ii is for indigenous.

Mexican food has great indigenous influence. The indigenous cultures of America cultivated *chile* peppers, corn, and beans long before the Conquest of Mexico.

What other foods are of indigenous origin?

Jj es para jamaica.
La jamaica es otra de las conocidas aguas frescas de México. Se hace de la flor del hibisco. Es de color rojo y tiene sabor parecido al del arándano.
¿Te gusta la jamaica?

Jj is for *jamaica*.
Jamaica is another of the well-known *aguas frescas* of Mexico. It is made from the hibiscus flower. It is red and has a flavor similar to that of cranberry.
Do you like *jamaica*?

Kk es para kiosco.

Un kiosco se encuentra en la plaza del pueblo. Sirve como lugar de entretenimiento o para servir comida en ocasiones especiales.

¿Has visto un kiosco?

Kk is for kiosk.

A kiosk or gazebo is found in the town *plaza*. It serves as a place for entertainment or to serve food on special occasions.

Have you seen a kiosk?

Ll es para pastel de tres leches.
El pastel de tres leches es un postre muy especial. Se prepara con tres clases de leche: evaporada, condensada y crema batida.
¿Qué otros sabores se les puede agregar?

Ll is for *tres leches* cake.
Tres leches cake is a very special dessert. It is made with three kinds of milk: evaporated, condensed, and whipped cream.
What other flavors can be added?

Mm es para mole.

El mole es una comida tradicional mexicana. Es una salsa espesa hecha del chocolate, maíz blanco y chile. Se usa para el pollo en mole. ¿Has comido el pollo en mole?

Mm is for *mole.*

Mole is a traditional Mexican dish. It is a thick sauce made from chocolate, white corn, and *chile.* It is used to prepare *pollo en mole.*

Have you eaten *pollo en mole*?

Nn es para nopalitos.

Los nopalitos se hierven y se fríen en aceite. Se les puede agregar huevo o camarones para preparar almuerzos o platillos de Cuaresma.
¿Has probado los nopalitos?

Nn is for *nopalitos.*

Nopalitos (tender cactus) are steamed and fried in oil. Egg or shrimp can be added to prepare breakfast or Lenten dishes.
Have you tasted *nopalitos*?

Oo es para ojarascas.

Las h/ojarascas se conocen también como pan de polvo. Se hacen en diferentes figuras como flores o estrellas. Se sirven en bodas y bautizos. ¿Qué otras figuras de ojarascas has visto tú?

Oo is for *ojarascas.*

H/Ojarascas are also known as *pan de polvo* or Mexican wedding cookies. They are made in different shapes like flowers or stars. They are served at weddings and baptisms. What other *ojarasca* shapes have you seen?

Pp es para pan dulce.

El pan dulce consiste en rica variedad de delicias como la concha, los cuernitos y las empanadas. Se vende en panaderías o tiendas de abarrotes. ¿Cuándo se acostumbra servir el pan dulce?

Pp is for *pan dulce*.

Pan dulce (sweet bread) consists of a rich variety of treats like *la concha, los cuernitos,* and *las empanadas*. It is sold in bakeries or grocery stores.

When is *pan dulce* usually served?

Qq es para quesadillas.

Las quesadillas se hacen de tortillas de harina con queso derretido. Las tortillas se doblan como tacos o se empalman y se cortan en triángulos. ¿Qué otros ingredientes se les puede agregar?

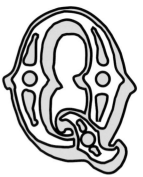

Qq is for *quesadillas*.

Quesadillas are made from flour *tortillas* with melted cheese. *Tortillas* are folded like *tacos* or made from two *tortillas* stacked together and then cut into triangles. What other ingredients can be added?

Rr es para raspas.

Las raspas son de muchos sabores como la piña y la cereza. Comúnmente, se compran en ferias y carnavales o de vendedores ambulantes.

¿Qué sabores les gustan más a los niños?

Rr is for *raspas.*

Raspas or snow cones are of many flavors like pineapple and cherry. They are usually bought at fairs and carnivals or from street vendors.

What flavors do children like the most?

Ss es para salsa.

La salsa se hace de varios chiles, tomate, cilantro y cebolla. Se acostumbra con muchas comidas. El pico de gallo es una de las salsas más populares.

¿Qué comidas se pueden comer con salsa?

Ss is for *salsa.*

Salsa is made from various types of *chiles*, tomato, *cilantro*, and onion. It is served with many dishes. *Pico de gallo* is one of the most popular *salsa*s.

What meals can be condimented with *salsa*?

Tt es para tortillas.

Las tortillas mexicanas son de maíz. Se usan para hacer tacos y chalupas. También se pueden comer las tortillas en lugar de pan.

¿Qué más se prepara con tortillas de maíz?

Tt is for *tortillas.*

Mexican *tortillas* are made from corn. They are used to make *tacos* and *chalupas*. *Tortillas* can also be eaten in place of bread.

What else is prepared from corn *tortillas*?

Uu es para uvas.

Las uvas se usan para preparar ensaladas y postres. En la cultura hispana se acostumbra comer doce uvas para recibir al año nuevo.
¿Tiene tu familia esta costumbre?

Uu is for *uvas.*

Grapes are used to prepare salads and desserts. In the Hispanic culture, it is a custom to eat twelve grapes to welcome the new year.
Does your family have this custom?

Vv es para vinagre.
El jalapeño con cebolla y zanahoria en vinagre
es un aperitivo popular en la cocina mexicana.
Se sirve con platillos de pescado y mariscos.
¿Has probado este aperitivo?

Vv is for vinegar.
Jalapeño with onion and carrots marinated in vinegar is
a popular appetizer in the Mexican cuisine. It is served with
fish and seafood dishes.
Have you tasted this appetizer?

Xx es para xícama (jícama).

La xícama es conocida como la papa mexicana. Es dorada o hervida como complemento. Se come también con chile y limón como aperitivo.

¿Cómo es la xícama?

Xx is for *xícama (jícama)*.

Xícama is known as the Mexican potato. It is fried or boiled as a side dish. It is also eaten with *chile* and lemon as an appetizer.

Can you describe *xícama*?

Yy es para yerbabuena (hierbabuena).
La yerbabuena es una hierba medicinal conocida.
Se toma en té para aliviar la congestión nasal.
Se le agrega miel y limón para mayor sabor.
¿Qué otros usos tiene la yerbabuena?

Yy is for *yerbabuena*.
Yerbabuena (mint) is a well-known medicinal herb. It is taken as a tea to cure nasal congestion. Honey and lemon can be added for greater taste.
What other uses does mint have?

Zz es para zanahoria.

La zanahoria se le puede agregar al caldo, al arroz y a las ensaladas. Además, se sirve como aperitivo en vinagre con jalapeño y cebolla.

¿Cómo te gusta comer la zanahoria?

Zz is for *zanahoria*.

Zanahoria (carrots) can be added to soup, rice, and salads. Carrots are also served as an appetizer marinated in vinegar with *jalapeño* and onion.

How do you like to eat carrots?

GLOSARIO FOTOGRÁFICO
Utensilios de la Cocina Mexicana

el cántaro

la cazuela

el comal

el jarro

el molcajete

el molinillo

PICTURE GLOSSARY
Mexican Cooking Utensils

la olla

el palote

la talavera

la tortilladora

el tortillero

la vaporera

AGRADECIMIENTO

Es con un gran sentido de gratitud que deseo dar reconocimiento por la colaboración y el consentimiento del Sr. Juan A. Mercado y Sra., del restaurante El Paraíso, al Sr. Romeo Mercado y Sra., del restaurante *The Steak House*, y al Sr. Roberto González y Sra., del restaurante El Rincón de los Ángeles, para usar fotografías de sus comidas mexicanas especiales en este abecedario sobre la comida mexicana. El compromiso de estas tres familias a la gastronomía mexicana es homenaje al trabajo y sacrificio de su madre, la Sra. Hortencia Medina.

También deseo dar mis sinceras gracias a mis amigas la Sra. Josefina S. Villarreal y a la Sra. Teresa Rodríguez por tan amablemente preparar sus especialidades para este libro en particular.

Finalmente, deseo dar reconocimiento, no tan sólo por la fotografía y el diseño de este libro, sino más importante aún, por el entusiasmo y esfuerzo de Maricia Rodríguez y Teresa Estrada en convertir esta idea en realidad. Es para ustedes, los niños preciosos, para quien les hemos traído la deliciosa cocina mexicana a sus salones de clase a través de este libro. ¡Es nuestro gran deseo que lo disfruten!

ACKNOWLEDGEMENTS

It is with a great sense of gratitude that I wish to acknowledge the collaboration and consent of Mr. & Mrs. Juan A. Mercado, of *El Paraíso* Restaurant, of Mr. & Mrs. Romeo Mercado, of The Steak House Restaurant, and to Mr. & Mrs. Roberto González, of *El Rincón de los Ángeles* Restaurant, for their permission to use photographs of their signature Mexican dishes in this alphabet book on Mexican food. The commitment of these three families to Mexican gastronomy is a tribute to the work and sacrifice of their mother, Mrs. Hortencia Medina.

I also wish to give my sincere thanks to my friends Mrs. Josefina S. Villarreal and Mrs. Teresa Rodríguez for so graciously preparing their special dishes particularly for this book.

Finally, I wish to acknowledge, not only the photography and design of this book, but, most importantly, the enthusiasm and the heart of Maricia Rodríguez and Teresa Estrada in converting this idea into reality. It is for you, the beautiful children, for whom we have brought the delicious Mexican cuisine into your classrooms through this book. It is our greatest hope that you will enjoy it!

SOBRE LA AUTORA

La Dra. Ma. Alma González Pérez es proponente de la educación bilingüe y dual. Es autora de varios libros bilingües galardonados para niños, entre ellos *¡Todos a comer! – A Mexican Food Alphabet Book* (Del Alma Publications, 2017). Nacida y criada en Ramireño, Texas, una pequeña comunidad rural en la frontera de Texas y México, la Dra. Pérez ha vivido en un verdadero mundo bilingüe y bicultural.

Entre los descubrimientos claves de su tésis del doctorado fue la relación positiva entre la proficiencia del español y el rendimiento académico. La Dra. Pérez fue profesora de educación bilingüe y directora del plantel de la Universidad Panamericana en el condado de Starr, el cual se especializa en el entrenamiento de maestros bilingües.

La Dra. Pérez ahora disfruta el escribir libros bilingües para niños, poesía en español, e historia local tanto como compartir su trabajo con maestros y alumnos a través del país. La Dra. Pérez, está disponible a través de www.dralmagperez.com para organizar presentaciones y talleres.

ABOUT THE AUTHOR

Dr. Ma. Alma González Pérez is an advocate for bilingual and dual-language education. She is the author of several award-winning children's bilingual books, among them *¡Todos a comer! – A Mexican Food Alphabet Book* (Del Alma Publications, 2017). Born and raised in Ramireño, Texas, a small rural community along the Texas-Mexico border, Dr. Pérez has lived in a truly bilingual, bicultural world.

Among the key findings of her doctoral dissertation, "The Relationship Between Spanish Language Proficiency and Academic Achievement Among Graduates of a Small High School in South Texas," was the POSITIVE relationship between Spanish language proficiency and academic achievement. Dr. Pérez served as an assistant professor of bilingual education and founding director of The University of Texas–Pan American (now UTRGV) at the Starr County campus in Rio Grande City, Texas, which specializes in the training of bilingual education teachers.

Dr. Pérez now enjoys writing children's bilingual books, Spanish poetry, and local history as well as sharing her work with teachers and students across the country. Dr. Pérez is available via her website www.dralmagperez.com for presentations and workshops.